# STELES

Other works by Tom Petsinis

*Fiction*

Raising the Shadow

The French Mathematician

The Twelfth Dialogue

The Death of Pan

Quaternia

*Poetry*

The Blossom Vendor

Offerings: Sonnets from Mount Athos

Inheritance

Four Quarters

My Father's Tools

Breadth for a Dying Word

*Plays*

The Drought

The Picnic

Elena and the Nightingale

Salonika Bound

Hypatia's Circle

# STELES

TOM PETSINIS

ARCADIA

First published 2019 by ARCADIA
*the general books' imprint of*
Australian Scholarly Publishing Pty Ltd

7 Lt Lothian St Nth, North Melbourne, Vic 3051
Tel: 03 9329 6963 / Fax: 03 9329 5452
enquiry@scholarly.info / www.scholarly.info

ISBN 978-1-925801-82-8

*In memory of my parents Vassa and Vasil.*

# CONTENTS

ΗΓΗΣΩ ΠΡΟΞΕΝΟ

# Saying Hegeso

As much as toes and fingers poised
To tell of journeys and parting gifts,
These thin letters, barely engraved,
Hold still the visitor's reflective eye –
Three short syllables fill the mouth
With the piquancy of winter quince,
Prodding the tongue grown sluggish
From daylong silence, unsealing lips
Parched by thirst and Athenian heat –
Voice cleared of foreign consonants,
A breath reserved for speech alone
Echoes, filling omicron with gender,
Restoring the word to womanhood:
Your name, spare, open, welcoming.

# Absent Epitaph

In the absence of an epitaph in verse
Commending how virtuous you were,
You're a young wife centred at home
Until the stranger whistled you away,
Or a mother, a newborn at one breast,
As evening grew darker on the other –
You emerge from the marble in relief,
A dream remembered in morning light,
Your gaze both here and down below,
Vacillating between calm acceptance
And a sorrow reason clearly restrains –
The proximity of death magnifies life:
Your leave-taking enhances the chair,
Legs curved finely to your soulfulness.

## Time's Touch

Time adds its own creative touch
To any work of art by taking away:
Picking in seconds, fading in years,
Observing the law that less is more –
Your once homely blues and greens
Have been reduced to autumn-grey
As befitting the nature of the scene –
Your eye, bleached of sea and sky,
And pupil that opened wide in love,
Stares with an appropriate vacancy –
Undyed by exposure to angled rain
Your dress is plain and becoming,
Its folds flowing over your stillness,
Rippled like the river to be crossed.

## Holding Nothing

Generations of shades brushing past
Have worn away the thing you held,
Its absence now a prized centre-piece
The sculptor couldn't have imagined –
Where once you raised in admiration
A crown of leaves pressed from gold,
Or a bracelet strung with amber beads,
Your profile, facing customary west,
Sees through all trappings and desires,
Intent on taking nothing when you go,
Neither a necklace's weight and shine,
Nor the pink impression left by a ring –
Your hands are graceful in emptiness,
Stranded fingers more eloquent in loss.

## Gold's Gravity

Intimate as a mirror held up close,
She continues serving to the end,
Her features reflecting your fears,
Breasts like pigeons poised to fly,
And dress, falling in simple lines,
But lacking the ceremony of yours –
Weighted with the gravity of gold
The box she places on your thighs
Presses you stiller in the moment –
She then tempts you in other ways:
The sudden shift of foot and knee,
Gathered hair smelling of smoke,
Flour and ash light on her sleeve
From baking for the waiting dead.

# Pandora's Box

You would raise the lid with delight,
Heart skipping at the choices inside:
The glow and shine to catch the eye
Of other women on the Sacred Way,
And in Athena's honour on the hill –
Today, though, you're circumspect,
As if choosing jewellery for another:
Amber to complement autumn light,
Or pearls to give roundness to tears –
And yet if this is your Pandora's box,
A nest where gold hatches its grief,
Look, a little hope also comes to life
And flies directly to your fingertip –
A bright ladybird spotted for spring.

# Opposing Forgetfulness

Caught in a flow of folds and curves,
You've already begun drifting away,
Your presence suggestive as a cloud
Slowly unforming in shades of white,
Becoming less body, more sentiment,
Growing each moment with the past –
To the girl in a moment of reflection,
Figure strengthened by straight lines,
You are the feel of the jewellery box,
Scent of lilac in a shawl left behind,
The heel's imprint in the leather sole –
By degrees her affection draws you
From the darker pull of forgetfulness:
You're leaning closer, about to stand.

## Crossroad: Kerameikos

It stands at a crossroad in Kerameikos
Where potters once turned clay to life,
But where now marble rises overnight
Like mushrooms at autumn's approach –
Citizens and visitors strolling this way
With a string of figs for the Parthenon
Pause to contemplate the homely scene –
Two women, mistress and young maid,
Profiles balanced, in permanent divide,
Their cheeks painted pomegranate red,
Stilled by the deft chisel in the moment
When deciding which jewellery to wear –
They continue, pensive, toward the hill,
More prepared to deliver their offering.

# Vanishing Point

Separation from earth has begun:
Too subtle for gravity's constraint
You would have risen like a cloud
But for the jewellery on your lap –
Resembling $\pi$, the chair's thin legs
Are tapered, pointing to vanishing
Under an imagined weightlessness –
Your left foot's already off the stool
And toes pressing soles with intent,
Firming for the space between steps –
Gold discs selected for their spirals
Will hang in stillness from your ears
As you depart with the procession,
Behind the muffled flute and drum.

# Ideal Proportion

An ideal proportion has determined
How your ear should rightly unfold,
Rules implicit to geometry protract
The obtuse angle of elbow and knee,
The forward tilt of head, neck, spine –
Before cutting back the slab to size,
The master-sculptor had calculated
The stresses between body and soul,
The tension sinewing beauty to bone,
The sublime ratio of length to width –
And so the finished rectangle frames
Your last, incommensurate farewell,
The irrational diagonal that connects
The eye's longing to the hand's loss.

## Transcendent Irony

Grief's the impulse for creation:
Orchestration of old hands ringing
Rhythm from hammer and chisel,
Colluding craftily to subvert time,
Conjuring a show of timelessness –
Your gestures lighten the gravity
Grained in marble blocked to size,
Your fingers peg ephemeral joy
As though a soft-winged butterfly,
Your forehead, unlined by thought
And too steep for skull-hard facts,
Reflects Athena in mantic attitude –
So, in a twist of transcendent irony,
Death's undone in the face of art.

## Across Millennia

Undated, your death draws us together:
Musician, sculptor, poet and foreigner –
Upright, the lyre is a bow in your grip
About to shoot notes across millennia –
Rhapsody sharpens the chisel to song,
Ripples the robe around lap and thighs,
Vibrates along the chair's slender legs
Down to the audience gathered below –
And you are still playing, now for me:
Contained by the frame your left hand
Is sounding a fifth on invisible strings,
Conducting this charge along my spine –
A tune from fingers spread in greeting
Or bidding farewell to your instrument.

# Perfect Harmony

Harmony of opposites observed:
Movement graced with meaning
Rising from surface counterpoint:
Youth, ever-spritely, light-footed,
Facing the seated wisdom of age –
The lyre's strings sounding wide
Against the range of vocal cords –
Hands knowing well in openness,
Others gripping the versed scroll –
Eyes guided by strict hexameters,
Others closed, imagining sounds –
A bent knee touching a still shin,
Left foot raised bare in rhapsody,
Crossed by another long and flat.

# Naked Rhapsody

Written on the skins of sacrificial goats,
Hexameters read unvoiced plod in lines
Like armed hoplites in regimental drills –
Words come alive, naked and incarnate,
In passionate union with lyrical strings –
With what purpose he unscrolls the text,
His vigour in delivering unrhymed verse,
Leaning back to project a voice arching
Over the old musician's head in a hymn
To the young who died challenging fate –
From this rhapsody of music and muscle
Athletes, full-flighted, oiled and shining,
Outrace their shadows in finishing first,
The fallen stand from murmuring blood.

# Disarming Time

So the musician outgrows the man –
Even seated on the customary chair
You dwarf youth alert to your tune,
Blind, expanding, eclipsing the sun –
Shaped for sound, your defined ear
Echoes the amphitheatre's rippling –
Fingers, the extremities of feeling,
Disarming time with a timely pinch,
Pluck, strum, commensurate caress,
Knowing the tension suited to epic,
Hymn, ode, improvised dithyramb –
His singing rises to a higher plane
As your foot taps stressed syllables,
Stamping its impression in the dust.

## Battle Dress

Stripped bare as a shadow on stone,
Cast adrift since her retreat began,
He needs a stronger sense of himself
To face the emptiness she will leave:
The helmet, sword, spear held tight,
The uniform's triple-layered weight,
Ground him upon entering her room –
She is more detached than yesterday,
Her stare unable to rise to his heart,
Yet, more by reflex than recognition,
She reaches for the hand he extends –
They meet, not in a grip, flat to flat,
Palms pressing the darkness to come,
Or the two coins warm in his sweat.

# Growing Indifference

With hearing now passive as your sight,
Sounds come as though from far away,
Your head turning neither right nor left,
Fixed between ears humming with wax –
Eyes open wider than the jewellery box
Your servant girl is rummaging inside,
Fingers tingling for the necklace or ring
That will satisfy Pluto's greed for gold –
Your child, naked, still unable to stand,
Reaches for your hem on chubby knees,
Crying for the breast still firm with milk –
Curled in the shadow under your chair,
The old cat purrs and twitches in sleep,
Dreaming of your hand stroking its ears.

# Dowry Piece

It hangs from your hand like a cloth
Left out overnight on a washing line,
Under a full moon struggling to rise,
Your fingers forgetful of their hold,
Forearm bare, rigid in a right-angle,
Slowing the still flow of your dress –
Was it placed on your maternal lap
By a relative muttering her farewell
In a custom older than reading ash,
The meaning discursive in smoke
Or is it from your oak dowry chest,
A handiwork that's never been used:
A fine weave embroidered with suns
For covering a face infernally dark?

# Turning Away

Made from oak with dark-eyed knots,
The thick-legged chair stood resolute
Throughout your full-term pregnancy –
Your body throbs as the nurse extends
The child wrapped tight between feeds,
Ready to place it on cushioned thighs –
A breast is loosened, heavy with milk,
When suddenly you turn from profile
To facing fully left, the shawl slipping,
Catching on a curl like a spider's web,
A maternal smile tugging at your lips –
Turn now away from the insistent cry
To a lone owl numbering the night sky,
Or a cricket struggling with your name.

# Unformed Thought

Three months of dreamless nights
And days when hungry echoes fill
Your ears like sea-sounds a shell –
The joy of motherhood has passed,
Now, empty after yet another feed,
You wrap the infant on your knees
And return it to the nurse's hands –
A thought, as yet not fully formed,
Still closer to a feeling than words,
Has overshadowed your happiness,
Growing above the sucking child,
Filling you with heaviness again –
You turn to the evening closing in,
Light slipping from the cypress tree.

# Diminishing Milk

The time for separation has come
But your words are still thoughts:
Take the drowsy infant to its room
Before the overbearing Parthenon
Spills its cutting shadow onto steps
And over walls whitened for spring –
I cover my head and dare not look
To lessen its attraction to my face,
The scent of my diminishing milk –
Oh, be a sister in this hour of need,
Loving mother to my embodiment,
For something is taking hold of me:
In feeding the child on one breast,
I feel its form growing on the other.

# An Afterthought

Between figures standing in full height,
Faces refined, restrained, in deep relief,
Arms angled in ease, covered and bare,
He is there only as a disembodied head,
A profile the depth of a passing shadow,
An afterthought etched in empty space –
But who is this sparsely-bearded youth
Whose features differ from the others?
(A servant has no role in this solemnity)
A grandson who fell later to the plague
That blackened temples and monuments,
Despite the calf lifted high for his sake? –
Look closer, his fingers are rising, bent,
As though to staunch his downcast eye.

# Grateful Son

There's no sorrow in his last farewell,
Only honour and his abiding gratitude –
He is taller than his father at this age,
Beard fuller, in the fashion of Pericles,
Standing proud of his democratic state –
Admire the surety with which he holds
The wrap draping his square shoulder,
And the steady gaze over the departed
At what he must manage and multiply:
Servants gathering big olives and figs,
Harvesting wheat fields up to his waist,
Dancing on grapes, slaughtering lambs,
Grooming horses to win at the Games –
His handshake is a seal promising this.

## Steadfast Wife

Her family, together in a confined space,
Though all strangely separate and insular:
Four fixed lines of sight that do not cross,
Each seeing death from a different slant –
She stands behind him, as custom insists,
As she has done throughout married life:
Giving him her breasts in mutual pleasure
And, in solitary pain, the son he'd longed –
Now, drawing aside the mourning shawl,
We see a profile chiselled finely by grief,
Lips set to whisper a composed farewell –
Her forearm rests lightly on his shoulder,
While the hand that knew where to caress
Is flat on his chest, yet not feeling a beat.

## Still Life

You cannot look the others in the eye,
Knowing they'd weep at your vacancy,
So, propped with one hand on the seat,
You follow with a still horizontal gaze
The memory of an evening at Sounion
With gulls flying low above a grey sea –
Yes, your preparations have been done:
Caressed by many hands with olive oil,
Sandals strapped tightly to upright feet,
Wrapped in the robe saved for festivals –
You are ready now to stand and depart,
Taking nothing but the touch of a palm,
The softness of breasts loosened in love,
The strength of the hand pulling you up.

# Remembering Now

The girl's disembodied head remains,
Facing the sun rising heavy with heat,
Left cheek comforted on a lined palm
As if nursing a tooth aching all night –
Caught in a moment of remembering,
She sees again, enlarged through loss,
Her mother, who died forty days ago,
Sitting on a chair with trunk-like legs
Carved from a disavowed walnut tree,
Preparing for Demeter's annual rites –
And she asks: where was I born from?
Her reply sounds again, together with
A smile and slight turn from the waist:
From between my dark armpit and rib.

# Fingers Firming

The departed are drawn by sorrow,
A thought away and almost palpable –
See how the grieving mother stands
(A servant would not be so familiar),
As if one body with her absent child –
She feels again with her very womb
The press of her dear daughter's arm,
The soft warmth of her womanhood,
While supporting a growing apathy –
And see how possessively she holds
The jewellery box against her breast
Covered in a cape heavy and coarse,
And her fingers, tender, unforgetting,
Firming to open the lid's gold clasp.

# Maternal Advice

And now her shawled head draws close,
As on that bittersweet, late-autumn day
When she whispered to the bride-to-be:
The necklet will complement your glow –
The groom came, horse sweating shine,
And took the girl away over five rivers
And one mountain range covered in oak –
As another groom waits on the doorstep,
Flipping two silver coins in killing time,
She picks the brightest pomegranate seed
And heaves a sigh for everyone to hear:
Take this, my girl, your true inheritance,
Keep it between your teeth with a smile,
So I might find you amongst the shades.

## Dead Centre

Centred between mother and child
Your gesture intimates a letting-go,
Like the poplar's indifferent shrug
At the drift and dance of its leaves –
Reclining on the high-backed chair,
You're in and out of time and place,
The curve of your body resembling
An hourglass left empty in the sun –
Leisurely extended, your arm rests
On a thigh once generous and round –
Renouncing both taking and touch,
Your fingers are pods poised to fall –
The evening waits to embrace you
In the garment gathered on your lap.

## Sorrow Restrained

A master sculptor, like an old midwife
Working sure-handed in fluid and flesh,
Extracting you fully grown from marble
Smoothed by a half moon waxing white –
His art, the subtle balance of opposites:
Sorrow restrained by a capillary of hope,
The lift from youth's exuberant curves
Against the pull of the rectangular grave –
And there you sit, poised as the goddess
Born fully armed high in the Parthenon,
And then too mortal in your torso's turn,
The angle of your knee about to extend,
A woman whose gracefulness emerges
From the tension between body and soul.

## Widening Space

The chisel was honed on heroic brows,
Lunar-cool limbs of nymphs and gods,
And all as practice, timely preparation
For grief now opening maternal hands –
The right is raised, tender and reserved,
About to caress the girl's ash-soft cheek,
The lifeline traversing her palm saying:
Look, *Thanatos*, how beautiful my child –
Her left supports the girl's weighty arm
Now reaching over the widening space
To keep herself from being pulled away –
Supports, but also a gesture of offering,
Saying: Here, carry her off, if you must,
But leave me her fingers' parting touch.

## Mourning Dress

She took them from the dowry chest,
Its dark grain flowing deep and still
Like the river that has to be crossed,
Its knots, eyes intense with suffering –
The dress and cloak spun from wool,
Woven on the loom whose clapping,
In time with the tap of wooden clogs,
Accompanied songs of love and loss –
She dyed them, hands black to wrist,
And hung them between olive trees –
With folds fixed, thick with shadow
A hundred times heavier than white,
They stoop her head and shoulders,
Her soles pressed flat to the ground.

# Preparations Done

She's been up all night with sister-owl,
Hair sprinkled grey from prodding ash
In preparation for the coming gathering –
The tunic, sleeves embroidered in blue,
And folded in thirds for a wedding-day,
Has had its last crease smoothed away –
Sandals, smelling still of virgin leather,
Will never be impressed by arched feet
Stepping on the drum's rhapsodic beat –
The pouch hanging empty on the waist
Held the discs that crimsoned her ears,
And that now stare from indebted eyes –
She will escort her, keening as they go,
Consoled by the whisper of myrtle trees.

# Waiting Groom

This was last done twenty years ago,
Her daughter was still not on her feet,
Now, instead of singing endearments,
She curses and heaves, if nothing else
To loosen this grief knotting her heart –
Mixing seven parts water to one wine,
She washes the girl from head to sole
And dries her stillness with the towel
Embroidered with pomegranate seeds,
Folded in three on her wedding night –
With her daughter dressed like a bride,
And the towel in the crook of her arm,
She sings again: It's time, dear child,
The groom's waiting on the other side.

# Servant Girl

As her faithful companion in sorrow
The servant girl saw to all her needs:
She bought sponges from the Agora
(The softest one could possibly find),
Raised dormant water from the well,
Went down to the cellar, urn in hand,
Broke oak branches on her bare knee
And fired the hearth with her breath –
This quietly done she now withdraws,
But apprehensive and curious at once,
Her fingers, not knowing what to do,
Reaching for her lobe soft and warm –
The intimacy of those grieving hands
Too bare for her to fully comprehend.

# Retreating Will

Sunrise trickles with a blackbird's song,
Thinning light loses its affirming touch,
A water-gourd's forgotten on the floor –
Your mother's letting-go surprises you,
As though she's now casting you adrift
In a seamless current becoming stronger
With your ebbing blood, retreating will –
As you reach out to her in apprehension
The tunic tightens, revealing your thighs
And accentuating the angle at your knees –
Your feet firm, toes curl, round heels rise
In readiness to push forward and stand –
The stool remains, grounded on all fours
Like a horse's hooves, opposing gravity.

# Low Relief

The marble was quarried on Paros,
Cradled here in a ship's ribbed hull –
It's commensurate with his sorrow,
White as a young dove's underwing,
So porous tears leave lasting stains –
Finally the sculptor has completed
Athena looking inviolate on the hill,
His hammer and chisel still warm,
The file with fine traces of wisdom
From a brow too steep for mortals –
He watches, his heart compounding
The only antidote to grief he knows,
Waiting for his daughter to emerge
In low relief from the veined stone.

## Second Delivery

From the hard shadow of the Parthenon
She calls on him, as though to a saviour:
Come down from the undeserving gods,
Assuage my heartache with your hands –
Please, deliver her to me a second time,
Draw my girl from marble's milkiness,
Restore her plumpness and good health,
Show her in the tunic I made last spring
Which draped her lighter than a breeze,
Intimating what she might have become –
Use your skill for the ripple in her hair
That would catch the unsuspecting light,
And show her sandaled foot in mid-step
As she would run to embrace her doves.

# Two Doves

Bowed by the weight of presentiment,
You're about to release a pair of doves
As though never to cuddle them again:
One, its clawed feet tight in your grip,
Has turned to you with an eyeless look,
Its wings lifting, poised to spring open
And scatter, clapping back in full flight –
The other, more round-headed, female,
You hold between bare arm and breast
Showing the first signs of womanhood –
It meets your gaze, knowing and calm,
Its beak, polished by the sun's steep rise,
Tasting the silence of lips pressed tight,
Or offering a seed from where it's been.

# Closed Hand

What meaning did the sculptor intend
Having the girl's hand closed like that?
Instead of holding still the lively dove
In a grip at once secure and solicitous,
She presses it awkwardly to her breast
(The tunic is incidentally gathered up
By the tail flat on her round abdomen),
Her wrist restraining a triangular wing
Pushing for the flock sweeping the sky –
Do fingers curl around an absent thing
(Pomegranate, mirror, doll-like charm),
Or does this gesture intimate the quick
Manoeuvring of birds, hands, underarm –
Both the paradox and possibility of art?

# Intimate Moment

You understand the language of doves:
The morning call of the repeated iamb,
At noon the courting coo in anapaests,
The litany of dactyls as evening comes –
And now, caught in your soft embrace
Like a lover you're destined not to hold,
It's set to peck open your uncertain lips
And confide all that it's heard and seen –
With hair brushed away from your ear,
Feeling the distances beneath its wings,
You're listening, head bowed, attentive –
Roads, rivers, countries yet to be named,
Your fifty-year future never to be lived,
All now on the tip of its consoling beak.

## The Tunic

She made the tunic over three nights,
On each an owl answered its own call,
The needle gleamed in her sure hand,
Eyes sharp in the lamp's steady glow,
Its oil pressed from olives pupil-black –
She'd wash it in water from the spring
And hang it in the plane's softer shade,
But only when basil scented the breeze –
Her tears fell like silver coins on stone
The day her daughter wore it lying flat,
Pleats undone, perpendicular to gravity,
And wears it still in the lowest of relief –
She sets milky figs at her parallel feet,
Shielding her eyes from morning glare.

## Against Gravity

Unweaned and still months from walking,
But having recently spoken his first word,
He hovers between sisters deep in thought,
Profiles shadowing the lime-washed wall –
Caught in this silence milked from sorrow,
The child's like a heartbeat held in palms,
A dove, at once alarmed, sprung in flight,
A narrow bridge across the years to come,
An offering raised to what cannot be said –
Unlike theirs his face beams in looking up,
Arm and fingers extended to full stretch,
His body pushing against grip and gravity,
Straining for tonight's cuddle, caress, kiss,
The curve of her breast just beyond reach.

# Two Sisters

Up, dear sister, return to your senses,
Father is chopping wood for the fire,
Mother has loosened her ashen hair,
Jackdaws have surrounded the house –
I couldn't raise you with the jewels
That brought rainbows to your eyes,
Nor with the gown stitched in gold
You shone in on your wedding day –
And so now I come with your infant
(Smell that blend of musk and milk?)
Whose crying reaches the Parthenon –
Up, dear sister, back to your breath,
Slip from the grip cooling your hand,
Mother this child with undying love.

## Post Natal

If you were sitting there alone
Your look would be mistaken
For the musing of melancholy,
Dürer's heavy-winged figure
Guarded by mute instruments –
But one unversed in epigrams
Might read signs of post-natal
Depression in the broken gaze
Seeing past the newborn child –
After taking in nine full moons,
The womb's sudden emptying,
Your precious innerness gone,
And then a giving of yourself
For the other's growing death.

## Body Language

Her presence there is only a conceit:
The crafty sculptor evoking sorrow
From a scene otherwise sentimental –
The right arm angled in acceptance,
Fingers curled under shadowed chin
In holding a pair of customary coins,
While the left hand's flat on her lap
And moving forward imperceptibly
As if preparing a place for her child –
One leg's drawn back under the seat,
The other extended casually in front,
Tightening the tunic over her knee,
The heel, round, unconditionally bare,
Is poised to slip off the low foot-rest.

# Telling Hands

In the absence of the figure facing them,
This could have been their first meeting:
Having fought with honour at Marathon,
(His broad chest is scarred for all to see)
He is now ready to serve again the state
In taking this young woman by the hand –
Her presence there sets a different scene,
A life-time later, both all-bearing mother
And sole witness of her fate, she reflects
On this moment more intimate than love –
The marriage grew from mutual respect,
To reading the light in each other's eyes:
He holds her now with a grip tightening
In gratitude, knowing he must let her go.

## Eternal Gratitiude

You brought makings to the marriage:
A dowry chest heavy with handicrafts,
Blankets composed on a naked loom,
This solid chair for breast-feeding on,
Pride in your thoughtful presentation
That welcomed relatives to the house –
And later you accepted your sacrifice:
The wound in giving birth to the son
Who would give his youth to the state –
Now you're exchanging deeper vows,
Taking nothing when you leave alone,
Except the charm-like pouch you hold
Discretely, arm extended on your lap,
And the press of his thigh on your knee.

# Still Birth

Full and round, glowing like sister-moon,
You prepared the clothes, cradle, dressed
This chair on which you'd feed your joy –
But other hands held her up still and blue,
And you've been sitting there ever since,
Waning, becoming thinner with each sigh,
Profile angled obliquely at its lowest ebb –
Deaf to doves gurgling in the walnut tree,
The boy calling for you down in the yard,
You bounce the buried infant on your lap,
Caressing the fine veins netting her head,
Weeping together with her crying for you,
Reaching for her fingers grasping the light,
Your breasts throbbing, painful with milk.

## Live Offering

Mother, you haven't looked up
Since your weight disappeared,
Or sat me on your lap and said:
How does a boy become a man?
I've brought a present for you:
The loveliest dove in the flock –
Here, hold it, you will improve:
This speckled band on its neck
Will bring a smile to your lips,
The push of its upturned wings
Will make your hands fly again,
Its strong, quick-beating heart
Will scatter those bad shadows,
Draw the sun back to your face.

## Facing West

Who are the dying and who the dead?
Where stands this couple staring west?
The spear he'd once thrust horizontally
Defending Athens from foreign attack,
Which lately served as a walking stick,
He now holds with declining strength,
And sure to collapse in a heap of bones
Without its support upright and fixed –
Not in the likeness of those on the hill,
Her face is a mother's, earthy, and set
With gritted teeth, defiant, not in grief,
And toes bare and bold under her hem –
Both are shouldering light's steep fall,
Their sights parallel, yearning to meet.

## Blue Vein

Maybe she slipped away like twilight,
Leaving her parents grey and destitute,
With a granddaughter for them to raise –
Even with head bowed, hair cut short,
Curled on rollers heated in the hearth,
She's still a tad taller than her mother –
Athena's face could have been drawn
From her rounded cheeks, curved chin,
Reticent lips sealed in a knowing line –
Her lowered gaze is tender with regret,
As if seeking her father's forgiveness
For darkening their old age with grief –
If only she could reach out to feel again
The blue vein on the back of his hand.

# Defiant Child

Is she the grieving mother's memory:
Her just departed daughter as a child?
Not bereft and profiled like the others,
She is figuring the future as it comes,
Front on, full-faced, a hint of a smile,
Imagining the woman she'd never be –
Another evening greys the Parthenon,
They're standing together on the step,
Her small hand safe in a stronger grip,
Wanting to pull away but still afraid,
Her left foot pushing forward timidly,
Wanting to join her friends in the yard,
To show them the mirror she's holding,
And her reflection nowhere to be seen.

ΞΑΝΘΙΠΠΟΣ

# Two Daughters

The daughters stand on either side of him,
Pressing close against his knee and thigh,
Dwarfed by the proud father he used to be,
Like when they were children and he'd sit
Before the winter fire warming his palms,
Telling them of Demeter and Persephone,
And they would listen, curious and afraid –
Now, left only with their memory of him,
They're alone in the space he once filled:
The elder, looking up and gesturing why,
Presenting a swallow for flight to his soul,
The other's hands are high in supplication,
Or perhaps about to sound a clap of grief,
Or catch a tiny feather falling from the sky.

## Bespoke Shoes

Your reputation flourished from your hands:
Complementing each other in tying a knot,
Threading a needle with a squint in its eye,
Cutting leather in curves for left and right,
Stitching them to soles for flat-footed poets
And high-arched runners with rounded heels,
As matching sandals for brides and grooms,
And boots that march dusty hoplites home –
Seated now, like Hades profiled on a throne,
You're admiring the cast flat on your palm,
Perhaps waiting for a pair of shapely wings
To push through the protruding ankle bones –
You smoothed the road to Eleusis for others,
Only to feel the dust beneath your bare feet.

# Future Bride

A girl, still playing with toys and pets,
Arms round and plump with puppy-fat,
Prepared overnight as a morning bride:
Hair curled by rollers heated in embers,
A band accentuating the brow's curve,
A tie beneath still undeveloped breasts,
The dress, with floral-patterned sleeves,
Falling simply, proper in parallel pleats –
Draped in immaculate black her mother
Curses the groom whistling in the shade:
Thrive on my daughter's unlived years,
Enjoy the full woman I'll never behold,
As for her free sons that won't be born,
They'll be slaves in your sunless state.

# Mating Call

Answering the gander's mating call,
You step out barefooted in the yard,
The sharp morning shadow normally
Preceding you now nowhere in sight –
Look, you say, raising in your hand
The naked Aphrodite from your bed,
Carved from scraps of the Parthenon,
And in the other, gripped just as tight,
A dove pushing for the circling flock –
Head high, the gander stands poised
As if to peck at the figurine's thighs,
A bag with flour hangs from the wall
And an axe-head with bevelled edge,
Waiting for tomorrow's fire and food.

## Age Difference

Being in profile your beauty is halved:
Slender neck, hair swept back in waves,
Stance light as ash from fire still unlit –
Suitors come from Thebes and beyond,
But you're mindful of the Sacred Way,
Eleusis, and the blush of pomegranates –
The little brother naked in your shadow
Substitutes for what lies buried in you:
Lively, thick-thighed, strong for his age,
The laurelled wrestler of future Games –
As he springs up from an angled knee,
Hands flying high for your votive dove,
Your thin-soled heel lifts stepping back,
Leaving him bereft, forever unfulfilled.

# Old Friends

Artemon, you've aged since last we met,
Your once robust chest is sharply ribbed
And sunlight now penetrates your beard –
Why the coarse winter-cloak, my friend,
When figs are still firm and milky inside?
How long have you held a walking-stick,
You, who marched to Marathon and back?
And where are you going, looking down,
On this dusty road through the cemetery?
Off to check your mares heavy with foal,
Or to pass a few hours with old Socrates
Chatting about immortality and the soul?
I won't detain you. Farewell, my friend –
But why is your hand colder than marble?

# Nightingale Revived

Unlike the Persians beating on drums,
The plague entered the city by stealth,
Palling the walled Parthenon in black –
Weakened by fever burning all winter,
Eyes deep-set and rimmed with purple,
You now step out in overcoat and boots
To a nightingale trembling in the yard,
The recent song frozen hard in its beak –
You warm it whispering endearments,
On breasts that milk will never enlarge,
Revive it with crusts from your mouth,
Until it grows stronger than your grip
And flies with your kindness to its nest,
Singing your sorrow in its mating call.

# Three Stages

Old age approaches from the right:
The slowing citizen loosely robed,
White-haired chest starting to sag,
A pouch alive with voting pebbles
Strapped around his thinning hand –
From the left, strict in iambic step,
Beard trimmed for death's festival,
Manhood, looking past the horizon,
Shield polished, defiant in its glow –
In the centre, youth, stepping light
Into the profiles' recollected space:
The day shining with oil and sweat,
Wreath more precious than a crown,
Trained body both muscle and soul.

## Light Footed

Your nakedness is natural as light,
A body sculpted by daily exercise,
Or what harmony would look like
If music were chiselled from stone –
As eternal laws unfold most vividly
In the forms and colours of spring,
So you're the embodiment of soul:
From the tilt of your lowered head,
Genitals hanging like a pair of figs,
To soles arched for bursts of speed –
The runner, beating the lean hound
To hares bounding fully stretched,
The thrower, intense, torso twisting,
The bronze discus eclipsing the sun.

## Winner's Glow

Pressed from summer's commonwealth
Concentrated in olives plump and black
The oil in the flask hanging by your side
Gives the tanned body its polished glow –
And after the winning jump, throw, race,
The flask's curved, bronze complement,
Shaped like a sharpened crescent moon,
Scrapes away the mix of oil, sweat, dust
Which vendors sell before the Parthenon:
The old use it as a salve for aching knees
And wrinkles becoming deeper each day,
The blind as drops for restoring the sun,
Losing athletes for stamina and strength,
And lovers of all kinds as an aphrodisiac.

## Athlete Reflecting

You set standards in three events:
The discus transferred your turn
To a parabolic arc record length,
Holding weights for added thrust,
You converted muscle to energy
In propelling to the longest jump,
Contestants followed your soles
Flying straight down the stadium –
After all this why so circumspect?
Does comedown follow victory?
Were you surprised by the silence
That filled the void between claps?
Or did you feel on bare shoulders
The shape of a cloud drifting past?

# Iconic Sorrow

Sorrow had never been depicted like this:
The chisel was fired in a furnace stoked
With blackest coal, bellowed with sighs,
Struck to the ring of iambic hexameters –
How deflated you appear on the bare seat,
As though having expended your breath,
Elbow fixed on knee, knuckles to cheek,
Your head, unthinking, tilted to one side,
Now only heavy with blood, brain, bone –
Caught in the downward current of folds,
Swirls, eddies, ripples, surging cascade,
Your child is falling, and eternally alone –
And you became the icon of all mothers
Mourning a son snatched from your love.

## Child's Play

Or maybe it's the sorrow of a mother
Resigned to separation from her child –
*Thanatos* has no meaning for the boy
(Its syllables still echo the sea at play)
Lounging back, casual between knees
Angled in the position of giving birth,
Head resting on breast no longer full –
He grips the hand supporting her head
To jolt her from her absentmindedness,
To focus her motherhood fully on him –
His other arm hangs loosely to one side
As though a wing spread wide in flight,
The pomegranate forgotten in his hand
Tempting the young cockerel to sound.

# Promising Talent

Yes, there's the reward that would come
From the investment of family and state,
But adolescence is the self-centred flame
Burning intensely for fame, not a beacon
Shining out for all who follow in distress –
Of youths selected to train in the palestra
You are the most singular and promising,
Modest, verging on shy, distant at times,
Shunning the crude practices others enjoy –
Your sole passion is the winner's wreath,
For which biceps harden pressing weights,
Chest broadens, abdomen parts in threes,
Thighs become stout and buttocks round,
To stay grounded against flesh and bone.

## Different Light

This is the day you've been training for:
Fringe trimmed and styled with fronds,
Cheeks shaved clean of growing down,
Ears still shapely, despite the headlocks,
And crimson with nervous expectation
As their cheering grows louder outside –
Now, about to disrobe for the oil's rub,
You're struck by the strigil's curvature
Defined by round biceps, thighs, chest –
In light's oblique, differentiating slant
It's an implement from when shadows
Were younger and still free of the sun,
Whose use your fingers cannot recover,
Despite nails cut too close to the quick.

## First Loss

Spring's burst was sudden but short-lived:
When winter bared its crooked teeth again
The almond-tree's blossom fell with snow,
Which you watched, pale with indifference –
You, the confident, strong-willed wrestler
Who stopped manly hearts, young and old,
By reserving your passion solely for fame,
Practicing feigns, holds, inescapable locks,
Breaking an opponent's grip with strength
Or slipping free with a sly, calculated trip –
Now you're caught in a challenging match:
Limbs unoiled, weakening, having no slip,
Breath labouring, body aglow with sweat –
You practiced for victory but never for loss.

# Elegiac Hands

Seven hands, all unassuming,
Unhousing a demanding fist,
Sinewed loosely to the wrist,
Seen not in the act of making
To satisfy some passing want,
Nor reaching for an oil lamp
To assemble souls home again
Scattered in the dead of night,
Nor showing what's to come
By the disposition of a thumb –
Seven hands, all renouncing
Yours and mine, open, giving,
Appealing to the god of five,
Enhancing hymns and elegies.

# Holding Back

Least able to endure the farewell,
The mother's standing at the back,
Where her sighing can't be heard –
A profile, and that barely a sketch,
Charcoal scratched on cold stone,
She looks away, pulling the shawl
Over her face, concealing the tears –
Firmer, more restrained, the father
Gazes over them at a cypress tree
Covered in evening's golden light,
Finding strength in his thick beard,
The other hand withdrawn, turned,
Desperate to reach out to the girl,
Knowing even a touch would burn.

## Sisterly Caress

Eight when suddenly the baby came,
She was old enough to help her grow
And teach her hopscotch in the yard –
Now twice the age the girl has lived
Her bust is heavy with womanhood,
Dress tight around softening thighs –
With parents dazed, drained of will,
Unable to undertake customary rites,
She now assumes her mother's role:
Misty gaze enfolding her like a veil,
Fingers caressing forearm and cheek,
Sighing before the threnody begins,
Whispering how beautiful she looks –
Breasts lifting in catching her breath.

# Faithfully Yours

This is how you might have looked
If you were upright on sandaled feet,
Filling the space sorrow has opened:
Hair cut and painstakingly groomed,
Jewellery on ears, fingers, thin wrist,
Dress and tunic crossed and centred
With a prized brooch between breasts
That will never develop and cleave –
The cape's hem folded in one hand,
Raising a small songbird in the other,
You appear to be asking your sister:
When will my soul spread its wings?
At which the woolly pup springs up
To the height of your covered knee.

# Stable Hand

Why such prominence in this work of art?
A man from the mountains of Macedonia,
Sold when a beard first shadowed his chin,
And after many years still not able to set
Both tongue and teeth in thwarting breath
To say the second letter of the city's name –
But here he is, returning at the end of day
From a forest thick with whispering oaks,
Or harvesting fields of waist-high wheat,
Implement in hand angled on his shoulder,
A look expressing more fatigue than grief,
In height now equal to the one he served –
Yes, he'll carry the flour for funeral bread
And stoke well the flesh-embracing flame.

# Prized Colt

As Xanthus wept when Achilles died,
This chestnut colt was just as prized,
Groomed by stable-hands to impress
And blind the high sun with its shoes –
It knew well the sound of your step,
Ears twitching when you approached,
Flanks quivering at each playful slap,
Knew your weight, your lift and fall
In time with its gallop, canter, walk–
And now, in expecting you to appear,
Its nostrils flare, eyes moisten, shine,
The front forelock up in anticipation,
Mouth open in readiness for the bit,
Or perhaps to neigh at your absence.

## Fortunate Citizen

A breeder of blueblood thoroughbreds,
Deserving winner at successive Games,
Patron of the Parthenon's equine frieze,
You walked the Agora in blue and gold,
Certain of the city's plague-proof walls,
Chewing a mix of fresh basil and mint,
Nodding, though more to left than right,
Here to Pericles, there young Praxiteles,
Resting for a while in the shade of a fig,
As Socrates, scratching his hairy chest,
Praised the beauty of the examined life –
Then home again, surrounded by vines,
Well-tended orchards and olive groves,
To enjoy your wine and a waiting wife.

## Fleeting Wealth

Where is your joy in possessions now,
The throb on seeing your favourite colt
That spurred the heart, quickened flesh?
Is that a look of sorrow or indifference?
Your hands are adjusting to emptiness,
Fingers, slender, tapering to effeminate,
Are withdrawn, feeling only the folds
Of a robe now more imagined than real –
At this instant are you moving forward
To a place behind fire, smoke and ash?
Or, mouth tightly sealed, stepping back
From what only shadows comprehend?
The proud height of the Parthenon rises
From the depth of silence and servility.

ΟΛΥΜΠΙΑΣ

# Rectangular Niche

Her body is set in a rectangular niche
Which could be a window, open door,
Or, if she's seen lying flat on her back,
The shallow sarcophagus whose ratio
Of length against width assuages eyes
That would otherwise well and weep –
The letters on the lintel have eroded,
But the line is still more than its edge –
The surmounting triangle is isosceles,
With, at its centre of gravity, a circle
Containing the triple-leafed cardioid –
A wing sprouts from the acute angles,
Fully spread, as though to fly her off
To forms transcending flesh and stone.

## Looking Out

Is someone approaching as night falls?
Rescued from the cat's triangular teeth,
The owl, tight against your chest, stirs –
Plump, round-faced, always chosen last,
Yet always blamed for the team's loss,
You endure their taunts looking down
At feet pigeon-toed beneath your hem –
Is it then the neighbourhood bully boy
Sneaking to frighten you with a prank
And sling names hurtful as bare stones?
Something more terrible seals your lips:
Maybe it's Athena levelling her spear,
Or Hermes in a cloak of cypress shade –
You hug the owl as though for dear life.

# Horizontal Gaze

She has welcomed relatives since dawn,
Serving boiled wheat and a cup of wine,
And now that all have left their respects
She enters the fragrant room last, alone –
The flame in the corner watches her step,
The table's set with three pomegranates,
Two silver coins, a marigold waiting still –
Her daughter is seated, palm flat on knee,
Staring as if dazed by the journey ahead,
The low footstool carved with half a heart –
She stares, unable to gather her thoughts,
Caressing the pale features with her gaze,
Until they reach out to each other at once,
Clasping halfway between death and life.

## Sublime Sorrow

Her farewell is less than a moment
(Millennia in marble's provenance),
Any longer and she would be stifled
By this sorrow arresting her breath –
A moment, profiles figured in space,
Shadowed by the lamp's vigilance,
And two hands strangely unfamiliar,
Barely accepting the other's touch
In this exchange of warmth and cold –
A moment, and she is present again,
Aware of what the other hand holds:
A cutting of pressed umbilical cord
In cloth saved for the wedding night,
Which she sets on the horizontal lap.

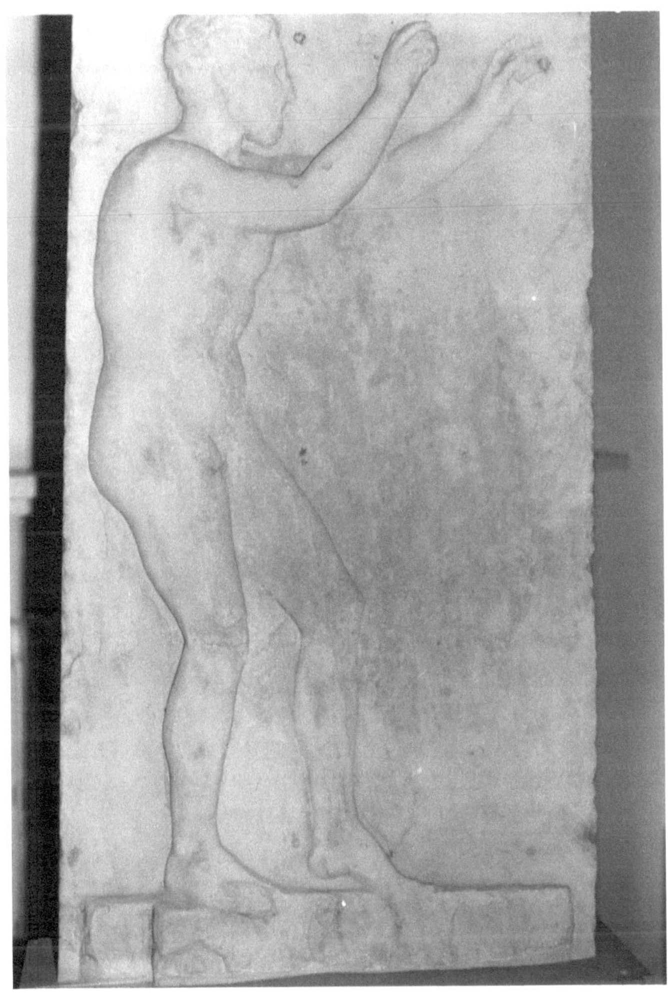

## The Wrestler

A gymnast swaying in balancing life,
Halfway between beginning and end –
Or a dancer moved by the dithyramb,
Hands raised for the affirmative clap,
Pivoting on one foot, poised to spring,
Turn in the air and slap the other heel –
As a celebrated wrestler you're both:
Stepping firmly on the palestra's dust,
Manoeuvring to grapple an opponent
The likes of which you've never seen,
Who, grounded, withstands your will,
Waiting to grip you in a stranglehold,
Pin your broad shoulders in surrender,
Leave with your heartbeat and breath.

# Hands Halfway

Two hands halfway between two hearts,
Between him and her, hope and despair,
One, thin-wristed, almost limp, held up
From falling by the other's tenderness –
As if from instinct or compelling need,
Both have only just reached out to clasp,
Fingers yet to firm in a purposeful grip –
Or is it the instant of easing and release?
Is it a shake in farewelling the familiar
Or a gesture in meeting again in a place
Where youth and beauty outlive stone?
Or perhaps they're pulling left and right,
Gently, with equal and considered will,
Enclosing a little darkness in their palms.

# Youth's Conceit

They're too young for husband and wife:
He's still an ephebe, aware of his looks,
Thin-necked, beardless, chest undefined,
She's a few years from full womanhood,
Small breasted, her knees casually apart –
Born into wealth, their profiles are alike,
And could be exchanged without taking
From the moment's solemnity and poise –
Is he the older brother stepping forward
With a milky fig or pomegranate seeds
She accepts covering his proffered hand?
Or is he Hermes, handsome in disguise,
In boots instead of his customary sandals,
Feigning sorrow, about to lead her away?

## Round Mirror

One hand extended in perfunctory farewell,
The other holding the round mirror raised,
Ensuring eyebrows are sufficiently arched,
Ear-rings complement the colour of cheeks,
The jaw-line's set with appropriate sorrow,
Thick shawl covers bare shoulders equally–
But then why is the surface turned like that:
The angle perhaps missing your reflection?
Afraid of looking back as twilight descends,
Are you observing another person's image,
A dark figure approaching from your right
Whose direct sight would turn eyes to salt?
Or is the mirror a measure of your presence,
Not blurring as you breathe out your name?

## Boy Dreaming

He watched from the edge of his boyhood:
The women, busy, dressed heavily in black
And crying like jackdaws at summer's end,
Men carrying the bundle wrapped in white,
After a slow start the fire's sudden upsurge,
The air thick with smoke, smelling strange,
*Thanatos* sounding with his brother's name –
And all the while he'd glance left and right,
Heart leaping at the sound of evening birds,
Listening for his whistle, awaiting his return
From hunting in the forest alive with game,
Imagining the hound bounding home first,
Partridges, rabbits, quail strung from a pole,
Heads swaying happily at his brother's step.

# Boy Waiting

Exhausted from the watching and waiting,
Eyes still teary from disembodied smoke
And straining to see through not-knowing,
He is sitting naked on the cold door-step,
Doubled over, thin limbs angled sharply,
His hand pressed between knee and cheek,
Drowsiness loosening his grasp on things,
Dissolving the women who've stayed back
To pick through ashes for something lost –
A dream of his own making draws him in:
He's unable to run from the coming bear,
When, from nowhere, his brother appears,
Composed, almost casual, larger than life,
Offering the firm protection of his thighs.

# Memory Fading

The woollen cape is coarse over his years,
His toes are numb despite the knitted socks,
Hair and beard left uncut since the funeral –
He often stops like this going to the Agora,
Or returning with consolation from a friend:
The sudden flutter of unease, breathlessness,
Panic at the tremor of approaching hooves,
Followed by disorientation, dearest thoughts
Scattering like leaves from a helpless tree,
Then the moment sparse with forgetfulness –
His hold on the aged walking stick tightens,
While the other hand, cold, adrift by his side,
Rises to the warmth of his mouth and chin –
A father unable to recall the face of his son.

## Faithful Hound

It howled in the courtyard long and low,
Scratching stones silver with moonlight,
Going back and forth between the pole
For tying game left shadowing the wall
And the sandals paired though opposite –
In the morning it trailed the procession,
Whimpering as women wailed in black,
Looking away from discarded footprints
At the bundle men were struggling with –
Now that flames have feasted and fled,
And the mourners returned to their lives,
It remains, moist snout sniffing the ash,
Eyes gleaming with growing expectation,
Ears poised, alert to the call of its name.

# Hunter Revisioned

As water assumes a vessel's shape,
Giving it fullness, ripple, radiance,
Perhaps the soul's attributes appear
Clearest in the naked body it moves –
A youth, lighter by an absent name,
Stepping from gold-hemmed robes
Like from disowned winding sheets –
Beauty in the shine of torso, limbs,
Abdomen tapering to prime genitals,
Grace in the curve of calf and foot,
Harmony in the knee angled at ease,
Transcendence in the sudden turn
Of the head in answering the future,
And eyes open wide to an inner light.

# Parting Smile

If you are not a soul turned inside out
Are you on the verge of becoming one?
You've already renounced the affection
Of those who'd keep you to themselves:
The dream in which the wishful living
Hunt the black boar following the dead,
Memories greying around the temples,
Straining to hold you with bow in hand,
The binding scent buried in oak-leaves,
Filling the forest with anticipated blood –
There's not a line of sorrow or remorse
For all those you're now departing from,
Only a smile about to show on your lips,
A butterfly moving marble to eternal life.

## Geomteric Calm

At ease, leaning cross-footed on a parapet,
Holding the knotted hunting-stick for poise,
You're recounting the day's catch and kill,
(Your father is listening, intent, each word
Prodding a heart heavy with presentiment)
When your profile turns suddenly full face
With a look more of knowing than surprise,
Eyes staring straight, with geometric calm –
Has the elusive stag appeared on the crest,
Head high, antlers cradling the setting sun?
Is that your girl raising water from the well?
Or, having finished the Parthenon's frieze,
Is the sculptor coming down to capture you,
For whom you've already shed your robes.

# Lyrical Gaze

Only those overflowing with youthfulness,
Or whom philosophy keeps young in mind,
Have the composure, confidence, strength
To whistle in walking through Kerameikos –
Athens was exuberant in her maidenhood,
Dancing to the dithyramb barefoot in dust,
Daring not only to turn her fears to tragedy
But to applaud blood-tears in the final act –
And so, having discarded your robe to show
An openness to whatever fate might bring,
You stand prefigured between your shadow
Older than flesh, cooling the blinding wall,
And your other self, still a vanishing point,
But growing with your gaze lyrical and long.

## Arched Foot

Overlooked when facing the sublime,
Your feet are ideal in their nakedness,
Shaped for pursuing an elusive dream,
Satisfying youthful needs and desires,
Realising beginnings, distances, ends
Which otherwise would never be seen –
Soles high-arched for yesterday's leap
Over shadow and stone, water and fire –
Heel raised above a ripe pomegranate
Left on the step in memory of the dead –
Toes lyrical as fingers pondering why,
Their lengths scaled in geometric ratio,
Curved to push back in going forward,
Bringing you here, to this place of rest.

## Backward Glance

Having defended the state seven times,
He prepares to serve as a hoplite again,
Despite wisdom turning his beard grey:
His shield polished bright on last night's
Moon glowing full above the Parthenon,
The spear honed slowly on a whetstone
Worn from bronze and blood gone hard –
Commanding a line of talkative recruits,
He looks up from his shadow in the dust
To the gorge filling with birds twittering –
He stops and glances over his shoulder,
Past the beardless youth pressing close,
To a cypress tree gold in evening light,
A thread of smoke unwinding his name.

# Battle Bound

He slept between arms presented by the state:
Warming the naked spear slender as a bride,
The sword double-edged, hard against his ribs –
In the morning they gathered to farewell him:
Father blessed the helmet with water and wine
And placed it on his head as though a crown,
Having counted silver tears smoothing creases
From his tunic, setting pleats with her palms,
Mother tied his waistband with a butterfly knot,
Then kissed both cheeks darkening with down –
And now, heel raised by this unexpected stop,
He wishes the old-timer would turn and march,
The sooner to fight and feast after the victory,
To carve the big-eyed lamb turning on the spit.

# Changing Forms

Masters in the art of manipulating marble,
Extracting figures from increasing depth,
Their hands able to suspend all disbelief,
(The dead farewelling a standing relative)
And conjure the semblance of movement
(A sinewed forelock raised, about to step) –
And even before commencing their work
They are able to imagine, intuit, foresee
Nature's undeniable addition to the scene:
Forms that shadows take in changing light,
Like the dreamy outline of Sounion beach
Rippling in a girl's hair loosened at night,
Or a beard grown youthfully black again
From an old man's long in wisdom white.

ΦΙΛΟΞΕΝΟΣ

## Taking Leave

In his sorrow, desperate to overcome
This invasion of his home by stealth,
He has armed himself like the youth
Who saved beloved Athens from ash,
Wearing helmet, breastplate, greaves
Against a sly foe mocking his sword –
When she appears, wrapped in shade,
Arms hanging, loose, as if sinewless,
Her gaze horizontal with his shoulder,
He reaches and takes her by the hand,
Resisting the darkness with his shield,
Determined to draw her back to light –
Her knee bends, moving opposite his,
Something stronger pulling her away.

## Light Touch

Who is dying and who's already dead?
Two suggestive figures barely in relief,
As if restrained from emerging in full
By propriety and the gravity of marble –
The master-sculptor's lightest of touch
Bowing a head, raising a hopeful heel,
Investing a dress with tension and fall,
A palm unlined and four fingers wide
With a gesture of greeting or farewell,
An eye with vision only for the other,
And lips printed with a lover's name –
All by scraping, caressing, smoothing,
Brushing away dust finer than pollen,
Creating a space for imagination to fill.

# Travel Advice

Are they parting from each other's breath
Or meeting after the last ember has died?
The woman's gaze is downcast, unseeing,
As if her sight's been pulled from within,
Her face a field abandoned to bare stone,
(Is this grief for herself or solely for him?),
Left hand clutching the corner of her cape
From fear she might otherwise drift away –
The man's grounded, more here than there,
His look more reproving than affectionate,
His gesture affirming the need for strength,
Advising: the soul we carry also carries us –
Their right hands are crossed, about to clasp,
Or perhaps having just loosened their hold.

# Night Offering

You lie awake on the verge of adolescence,
New thoughts growing of their own accord
Like long hair loosened before going to bed –
A pomegranate falling in the growing dark
Thumps between your undeveloped breasts –
In the morning, accompanied by jackdaws
Sounding from poplars showing their limbs,
You set out briskly for the night's offering,
Yard damp with dew under soles worn thin,
Dress unbelted in your haste to be there first,
Undulating freely from the shoulder clasp –
The breeze rustles leaves shaped like hearts
Over the lined games drawn on the ground,
Standing the down on your sleeveless arms.

# Two Pomegranates

After the figs that sweetness burst ripe,
You're drawn to the season's final fruit
On soil soft from shade and recent rain –
One's large, its leafy stem still attached,
And heavy with unscented inwardness,
The other smaller, split by a thin smile
Which, for an instant, catches your eye
And high-arched foot midway in stride –
Skin shining with the summer to come,
Bright as the cheeks of girls you admire,
Seeds like beads defining their breasts –
Last night's dim presentiment becomes
Your fingers in morning light, this find,
The neat depression stamped by its fall.

# Details of Steles

www.ingramcontent.com/pod-product-compliance
Ingram Content Group Australia Pty Ltd
76 Discovery Rd, Dandenong South VIC 3175, AU
AUHW020135130726
429791AU00003B/119

9 781925 801828